3D SNAPSHOTS SAFARI ANIMALS

3D SNAPSHOTS SAFARI ANIMALS

FOG
CITY

PRESS

Published by Fog City Press,
a division of Weldon Owen Inc.
415 Jackson Street
San Francisco, CA 94111 USA
www.weldonowen.com

WELDON OWEN INC.

President, CEO Terry Newell
VP, Sales and New Business Development Amy Kaneko
VP, Publisher Roger Shaw
Executive Editor Elizabeth Dougherty
Managing Editor, Fog City Press Karen Perez
Editorial Assistant Katharine Moore
Associate Creative Director Kelly Booth
Designer Michel Gadwa
3D Illustration Andy Lackow
Production Director Chris Hemesath
Production Manager Michelle Duggan
Color Manager Teri Bell

Text Maria Behan
Picture Research Brandi Valenza

A WELDON OWEN PRODUCTION
© 2010 Weldon Owen Inc.

ISBN 978-1-61628-054-3

10 9 8 7 6 5 4 3
2014   2013   2012

Printed by RR Donnelley in China

What are safari animals?
Well, a safari is a journey, so
safari animals are creatures
that are so special, they're
worth taking a trip to see.

The animals you'll find in this
book are from Africa, and for
many of us, Africa is very far
away. But by turning the page,
you can start out on your own
safari—a journey where you'll
meet some amazing animals!

On the plains
of Africa, animals
will often travel
in a group.
A group of zebras
is called a herd.

Sometimes, you find animals on their own, but most of the time, they stick together.

Animals often hang out with their own kind. But sometimes, very different creatures team up, like hippos and birds.

Young animals learn from the other members of their families, just like we do.

Baby animals
usually stay close
to their mothers.

It's good for
young animals
to explore a bit,
though. It helps
them pick up
new skills…

...like jumping,
flying, and
roaring!

Africa is home to many beautiful birds. These pink flamingos look like bright flowers blooming in the green grass.

Some African birds have red faces and striped wings, and others have head feathers that look like fancy hats!

What does this leopard see way up high? A bird? Or maybe a monkey?

Or even a giraffe?
Thanks to their
l-o-n-g necks,
giraffes are way
up high even
when they're
standing on
the ground!

Some animals have large ears so they can hear the things going on around them.

These animals
have a great
sense of sight,
which is handy
for hunting
or just getting
around in
the dark.

Other animals
have grand
horns that
they can use
for wrestling
or breaking off
branches to
reach leaves.

Cheetahs are beautiful when they're at rest, but when they run, they are just a blur. Cheetahs are the fastest animals on Earth. They can run up to 75 miles per hour (120 kph)!

Safari animals hunt in different ways: some use sharp teeth, some squeeze with a tight grip, and others grab with strong claws.

With teeth like
these, it's hard to
believe this monkey
eats mostly fruit!

Animals that eat meat—like caracals, wild dogs, and hyenas—have strong teeth and jaws. The better to bite with!

Other safari
animals are
gentle plant
eaters, happiest
when they have
some tasty
grass or berries
to munch.

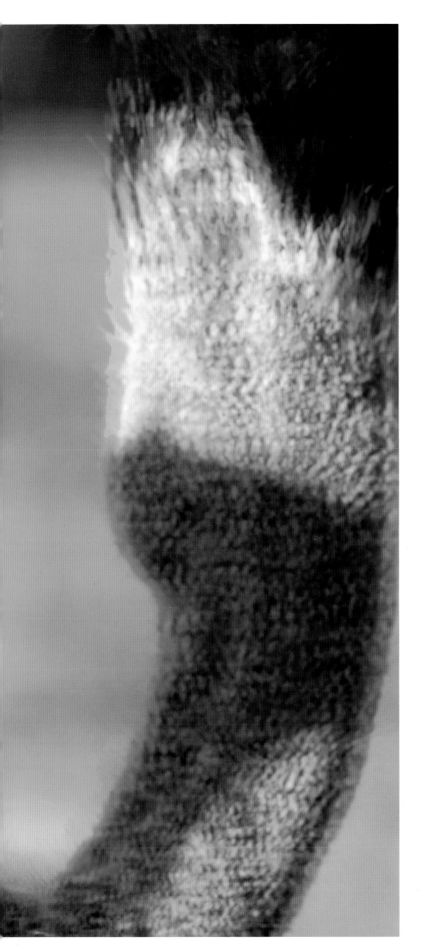

Ostriches eat creatures like bugs, but their favorite treats are nice, tasty leaves.

Animal meals are as different as the creatures eating them. But Mommy's tail is not food—ouch!

Many African birds—and some creepier creatures— spend most of their time in or near the water.

Hippos make splashing around in the water look like fun, don't they?

Much of Africa is dry, so animals drink wherever they're lucky enough to find some water.

Hunters and people moving
into natural environments cause
problems for these animals.

Some animals that were once common across Africa now live in only a handful of places.

But if people work together, we can keep these wonderful animals part of our world for a long, long time!

African Wildcat
Africa and the
Middle East

 Meerkat
Southern Africa

 Secretary Bird
Sub-Saharan Africa

 Warthog
Sub-Saharan Africa

 Guinea Fowl
Sub-Saharan Africa

 Crowned Crane
Sub-Saharan Africa

 Baboon
Africa

 Warthog
Sub-Saharan Africa

 Osprey
Worldwide except
Antarctica

 Zebra
Eastern and
Southern Africa

 African Lion Cub
Sub-Saharan Africa

 Black and White
Colobus
Central and Eastern
Africa

 African Fish Eagle
Sub-Saharan Africa

 African Elephant
Sub-Saharan Africa

 Leopard
Sub-Saharan Africa

 Blesboks
Southern Africa

 Serval
Sub-Saharan Africa

 Giraffe
Sub-Saharan Africa

 White Rhinoceroses
Southern Africa

 Puku
Central Southern
Africa

 Hare
Africa

 Zebra
Eastern and
Southern Africa

 Secretary Bird
Sub-Saharan Africa

 Greater Kudu
Eastern and
Southern Africa

 Wildebeest
Eastern and
Southern Africa

 African Lion
Sub-Saharan Africa

 African Wild Dog
Sub-Saharan Africa

 Hippopotamuses
and Egrets
Sub-Saharan Africa;
worldwide except
Antarctica

 Flamingos
Africa, Asia, and
the Caribbean

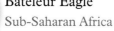 Leopard
Sub-Saharan Africa

 Hippopotamuses
Sub-Saharan Africa

 Bateleur Eagle
Sub-Saharan Africa

 Bush Baby
Sub-Saharan Africa

Osprey
Worldwide except
Antarctica

 Brown Hyena
Southern Africa

 Hippopotamuses
Sub-Saharan Africa

 Kudu
Eastern and
Southern Africa

 Gazelle
Africa

 Giraffe
Sub-Saharan Africa

 Red Hartebeest
Southern Africa

 Blue Duiker
Central and
Southern Africa

 Yellow-Billed Stork
Eastern Africa and
Madagascar

 Nyala
Southern Africa

 Defassa Waterbuck
Sub-Saharan Africa

 Black-Backed Jackal
Eastern and
Southern Africa

 Cheetah
Sub-Saharan Africa

 **Ostrich**
Africa

 Bontebok
Southern Africa

 Serval
Sub-Saharan Africa

 Ground Squirrel
Worldwide except
Antarctica

 African Elephant
Sub-Saharan Africa

 Rock Python
Sub-Saharan Africa

 Crested Grebe
Europe, Asia, Africa,
and Australia

 Lowland Gorilla
Western Africa

 African Fish Eagle
Sub-Saharan Africa

 African Elephant
Sub-Saharan Africa

 Nile Monitor Lizard
Sub-Saharan Africa

 Vervet Monkey
Sub-Saharan Africa

 Great Egret
Worldwide except
Antarctica

 Warthog
Sub-Saharan Africa

 Caracal
Africa, Western Asia

 Flamingos
Africa, Asia, and
the Caribbean

 African Lion
Sub-Saharan Africa

 African Wild Dog
Eastern and
Southern Africa

Nile Crocodile
Sub-Saharan Africa,
Madagascar

Flamingo
Africa, Asia, and
the Caribbean

ACKNOWLEDGMENTS

Weldon Owen would like to thank the following people for their assistance in the production of this book: Lucie Parker, Phil Paulick, and Heather Stewart. 3D Conversions by Pinsharp 3D Graphics Liverpool UK.